MW00636835

THE ORACLE ON

SMOKE

**BEING *A* FEW UTTERANCES IN *A* SIM-
PLE AND NOT *AT* ALL DELPHIC
STYLE, WITH CERTAIN SO-
CALLED POEMS THERE
AMONG SCATTERED**

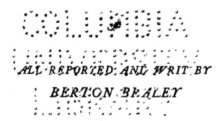

ALL REPORTED AND WRIT BY

BERTON BRALEY

Madison, Wisconsin
1905

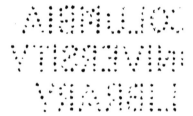

Published by The Sphinx
Printed by the Parsons Printery

TO

MY MOTHER,

WHOSE CURTAINS I HAVE SCENTED,

AND WHOSE

PATIENCE I HAVE TRIED

. FOR

MANY YEARS

WITH

MUCH SMOKE;

THIS BOOK

IS

JOYFULLY DEDICATED.

.

AT THE THRESHOLD

Two of the Oracle's Talks ('On the Pipe' and 'Sans Nicotine') as well as some of the verse, have appeared in the Sphinx at divers times.   The other matter herein appearing has never before stood in type.

In all of it there is no purpose save to amuse the smoker and give a genial word for man's devotion to the weed, "which combines the venom of the serpent with the compassion of the prophet."

And that no one may unjustly accuse me of "borrowed ideas," I protest now that I have never read "My Lady Nicotine."

B. B.

THE ORACLE ON CIGARS

"Undoubtedly," said the Oracle, after he had passed us all the cigar box, and was settled back in his ragged Morris chair, "undoubtedly I am fully qualified to dissertate on the cigar in the most appreciative style, for I so rarely am fortunate enough to have a fat brown weed that my appreciation is enhanced by long abstinence, and therefore, perhaps without warrant, I am prone to consider the cigar as essentially a festive luxury, something that goes with five course dinners and a feeling of contented repletion.

"On such an occasion a fellow lolls lazily back in his chair with his legs clear under the table, unbuttons his vest and gazes on life through an aromatic, bluish haze which throws a glamor over all things. The world's all right, life's worth living, success looms large through the smoke, and the earth is but a plump cigar which you hold between strong fingers and from which you draw contentment and plethoric dreams. You never noticed before how kindly and genial are all the men in the room. That man Brown whom you've always felt to be an ass is really not half bad, and that story he's telling has a new glint of humor in it, a gleam of fun which you never noticed on the ten previous occasions when Brown told it.   And Perkins, dissipated and profane Perkins, whom you've always detested, why now that you study him through the smoke, seems quite a different fellow; you feel certain that half the tales about him are mere venom from his enemies, and you experience a certain slothful indignation that so fine looking a man should be thus maligned.

" Wrapped in the cloud of Nicotinian fragrance as you are, you acquire for the time a certain easy tolerance and kindly sympathy which make you kin with all mankind.

" I have seen sworn enemies, rivals in business and love, society and politics, men who can say nothing bitter or acrid enough about each other ordinarily,— I have seen such men, when thrown together by chance in the same smoke-filled room, melt from sullen silence to plastic composure, and so finally to smiling conversation with the very men they so long have tried to incinerate in the furnace of their hatred.

Probably the next day will see them the same fleering foes as usual, but that they for even a little space foregathered in concord must be written fair for the magic of the cigar.   Sharp lines blur in smoke, sharp prejudices and animosities soften.

" Therefore, to gain the full benefit of a good cigar, one

should have eaten well and be among his kind. Thus at least it runs with me; I glean no dreams of future or past from a cigar; I build no castles in its smoke, but I become instilled with a sense of loafing tenderness and warm comradeship, with a glow of love and — but I am only repeating myself. Not for long will this box of brown beauties endure,.and when they have taken to themselves wings of blue smoke and fled into the circumambient ozone, the gods alone are 'ware of when I shall have another box. Which means in simple United States, that 'Lord knows when I shall get another.'

" Let us therefore enjoy the Gift of Fate to the uttermost and waste no more smoke-scented moments in babble. There still remain a few cigars and I would have you each take another. Here, fellows."

And the crowd continued, as the Oracle became,— silent.

WH.EN THE SMOKE'S A' CURLIN ROUND

WHEN the " shades of night have fallen," an' the window shades have too,
When the radiator's hissin' as the steam goes chuggin' through,
An' its comfy to be sprawln' in yer ragged easy chair,
Just to lie at ease and listen to the sounds about yuh there,
When ye're sort'a kind'a drowsy and yuh ain't a carin' much,
'Cept to lazy there a dreamin' dreams of happiness an' such;
Then a feller sort'a lows he likes to be a " lazy hound,"
An' to watch his pipe bowl gleamin' while the smoke's a' curlin' round.

An' yuh lie there just a thinkin' thoughts as hazy as the smoke,
Of the things yuh'd be a' doin' if yuh weren't so rotten broke,

An' yer eyes is busy blinkin' at yer "Castles built in
  Spain,"
Though they tumble down in ruin yuh can always build
  again;
Then yuh get to kind a' rakin' up the things of long ago,
Things yuh thought yuh had forgotten, till yuh see them
  come an' glow
In the bluish mist ye're makin'—there's philosophy pro-
  found,
In yer memories an' plottin' when the smoke's a' curlin'
  round.

So outside yuh let men bicker, buy and sell, an' rise er fall,
While within yuh watch the changes in the smoke cloud
  over all,
Watch the visions shift and flicker, see the faces form and
  fade,
As yer foolish fancy ranges in the dreamland yuh have made.
Where is trouble, pain or sorrow?   Here is nothing only
  peace;
For the hosts of care must falter an' the little worries cease;
They may deafen yuh to-morrow but to-night they make
  no sound,
Silenced at tobacco's alter, while the smoke's a' curlin'
  round.

A PIPE TALK

"A pipe," said the Oracle, as he filled his from a jar on the table and borrowed a match from MacPherson; "a pipe is the only proper smoke. To me, the essence of smoking is its comradeship, and comradeship requires individuality. Now there's individuality to a pipe, there is none to a cigar or a cigarette. A pipe gets to be an old friend, it has a personality, a history, and when you smoke it you feel as though you were talking over old times with a tried and staunch old comrade.   How much you two have gone through together, you and that scorched briar.   Remember that time when you were in the logging camp, that's when that little nick in the stem got there; then the jagged scratch on the bowl came when you were so nearly killed in that runaway.   You look into the bowl and notice for the five hundredth time the place where you pried off a bit of the 'cake' to show Her how much the pipe had been smoked, and you smile reminiscently as you remember how She held up Her finger at you and said, 'You naughty boy, I'm afraid you smoke terribly.'

"And you count the little dents in the pipe, which appeared that day you threw it out of the window and vowed you would quit for good, while you grin gleefully, recalling how you chased out the next morning and hunted for two hours until you finally found your strong old comrade and danced with joy at your success, and swore you'd never quit again until you died.

"But memoried joys are not the only ones found in a pipe.   It gets to be almost a part of you as well as of your history.   How the stem settles itself comfortably in its own space between your teeth, how the bowl grows warm and shining in your supporting hand, and if it is a 'bulldog' how it nestles against your chin, as if it belonged there — as it does.

"A pipe has moods, too — it is almost human in them. Don't you know how it sometimes gets unaccountably rank and bitter, and how, though you clean it and pet it and pamper it with the mildest and sweetest of tobacco, it still remains stubbornly ill-tempered?

"Then you lay it aside a bit, and behold it stops sulking and becomes cheery and pleasant again. And sometimes it takes on a glorious good humor which even the worst tobacco cannot disturb, and then smoking it is verily 'the crown of pleasure,' for it soothes and caresses, and warms the cockles of your heart with its rich and glowing sweetness.

"I have seen the world somewhat, my children" and the Oracle smiled benignly upon us, "I have tasted life and its joys, I have known the fierce pleasure of combat and the intoxicating glory of success, but at the last I find, to quote my own famous verses:

'I sought my heaven in books, and found but dust;
'I sought for it in fame, and found but power;
'I followed fortune and received a crust;
'Love's gift to me was but a withered flower,
'And then, my wisdom with the years grown ripe,
'I sought my heaven and found it — in a pipe.'"

THE ORACLE SANS NICOTINE

"Dances," said the Oracle, reaching mechanically for his pipe and then settling back into his chair as he remembered that he had sworn off, "are a convenient method of going broke; they are —"

"You said that last night, Oracle," interrupted the Engineer, "for heavens sake give us something new; it's bad enough to listen to your futile burblings anyhow, and when you begin to repeat —"

"Well what if I do," said the Oracle, irritably, and the gang looked startled, for the Oracle was wont to be serenely oblivious to criticism, "it's worth repeating, which can't be said of the puerile twaddle you usually manufacture as conversation. Now you choke off or I'll hand you a good stiff one in the laths;— Dances are a convenient method — hang it, Peters, quit twiddling your thumbs! you'd drive a camel to drink! Bangs, can't you leave your watch chain alone? You fellows get on my nerves with your eternal fidgets!"

It was plain that the Oracle felt nervous and we wondered.

"Oracle," ventured the Engineer, tentatively, "why

is this whichness? Whither has fled thine old time insouciance? Wherefore — ''

'' Oh head in on that archaic rot and — damn it; Peters, if you can't keep your foot still for at least one second, cut it off! You all act like a lot of uneasy angle worms! Where was I at? Oh yes, dances are a con —''

' Fidence game on the unwary bachelor,' — say that for the sake of variety, Oracle, the other is somewhat hackneyed and —''

'' Say, I wish you fellows would reserve your facetiousness for the eager ears of your super-educated friends. I for one find my rude and undeveloped intellect unequal to the strain of following your subtleties. — Ticks, why the deuce don't you clean that pipe in your own room? Do you think I can sit here and watch that nauseating — Say Bangs, imagine you have the tetanus for ten seconds, and desist from that mastication of tooth-picks; you've got more senseless, foolish, childish, infantile, idiotic mannerisms than any one I ever had the misfortune to know! Ugh!

'' Well, to continue — dances are useful and democratic institutions; that as a general statement, requires elucidation, and my arguments based upon this postulate unfold much as follows —''

The Oracle paused, malignantly gazed at the Engineer who was drawing tit-tat-toe marks on a calling card, and then reached for his pipe, filled it, lit a match, but remembering his vow, laid the companion of his heart aside, and wearily sank back in his chair.

"Fellows," said the Oracle, "smoke up! I may have quit, but I want to catch the old homely whiff of Durham again, for I have been marooned on the altar of self-sacrifice overlong. I guess maybe that's why everything makes me jump like a hair-spring charged with electricity."

The scent of burning tobacco from three pipes and two cigarettes floated across the room to the immolated Oracle, and his eyes closed in beatific peace. Then he reached guiltily for his pipe and put it in his mouth. "Just a dry smoke, boys," he said in an unconvinced sort of tone, and the gang winked portentously, "Let's see, where was I? oh yes; arguments unfold as follows —"

There was the rasp of a match and Bangs held the blazing bit of pine just above the Oracle's pipe; the Oracle shook his head, but his eyes hungrily watched the flame eat along until only an inch of the match was left, and then his left eyelid slowly slid down over that eager orb and he drew deeply and joyously on the battered mouthpiece of the pipe as Bangs dropped the still burning match on the charred bowl. The Oracle blew a cloud of smoke at the pipe rack just above his chair.

"Smoking," said the Oracle, with a luxurious sigh, "is the habit of Philosophers."

"But go on with your dissertation upon Dances" said the Engineer, graciously.

"Dances" quoth the Oracle, "are to be danced, not philosophised upon."

WHIFFS FROM THE ORACLE'S CIGARETTE

"As a man of the world," said the Oracle, rolling his ninth after-supper cigarette, "I am aware that a prejudice against these dainty tubes exists, but as a scientist and a cigarette smoker I believe it my duty to defend the much-attacked 'coffin-nails.'

"And in doing this I shall disregard all the puerile accusations so often burbled forth, and expatiate only on the virtues of the 'dude stick,' as crack-brained adversaries vapidly term it. There come times in every man's life when a short smoke is a thing most avidly to be desired, yet when a pipe would be a reeking offense and a cigar a riotous extravagance; what then? shall the hankering mortal still hank or shall he take the 'making's' or his case from his pocket and inhale a few heaven-savoring whiffs? Surely the latter, for thus shall he save himself from the nervous grouchiness of self denial, or the folly of a cigar four-fifths wasted.

"Then for the man who rolls his own smokes there is a certain pride of workmanship in creating them when he is alone, and a certain time filling pause in constructing them when he is in the throes of 'fussing,' which compensate for many ills whose parentage is laid to these 'boy killers.'

"And when She, with dainty but unskilled hands, strives to roll a real cigarette for you, what a smile of absorbed anticipation and condescension overspreads your face, and ho ambrosial to the taste and aromatic to the nostrils is the limp and amatuerish product of Her endeavor. Then you begin to roll another with consciously unconscious ease and you swell up mightily when She says, ' Oh how cleverly you do things! why it looks just awfully easy, but I can't seem to make them at all.'

" Of course you proceed at once to tell Her, ' it's just a matter of practice, you see I smoke so much that I can't afford to buy made cigarettes, in fact I believe I smoke *too* much,' proving this assertion by a display of much yellowed fingers at which she inveighs n half awed disapproval.

.   .   . " But after all, with me at least, it is in the quiet of my room, when my brain is fagged and my pipe gone foul, that I love the cigarette best. There is such lolling content in merely watching the thin band of smoke which streams up from the burning end, and such lazy acuteness in noting how the thread like smoke from the paper curls itself into intricate filigree work as it gets away from its source, and how the blue from the tobacco breaks from a ribbon into a formless hazy cloud and then melts into nothingness.

" The dreams and reveries that come to me with a cigarette are those only of past delights and follies, of dances and flirtations, of whispered nothings and easily won and lightly given kisses, of frivolous and fickle maids whose eyes have sparkled for me, and of all the airy frip-peries that have sprightlified existence.

"With a pipe I will dream of comradeship and work and sorrow, of pain borne patiently and joy won through toil and struggle,— a cigarette brings back only the dreams that are trivial, though smile-suffused.

"But the final canonization of the cigarette, the most abso-lute fitness in its use, is when it gleams in a woman's hand or between her lips.

"No Puritan I.   Let the woman be piquant, pert and pretty, let her be gowned in taking wise, and let her smoke only the best Egyptians with her monogram in gold thereon, and I will fall down and worship.   If it please her Majesty to blow fragrant rings and aureolize her beauty in a mist of smoke, I will respect her none the less, and if she wafts graceful exhalations from temptingly pursed up lips and with a languorous deftness I will proclaim her the apotheosis of the smoker.

"As my friend Horatio Winslow says, a little too rakishly perhaps,

> ' She hates conventionality,
>   She's different from the rest,
> She scorns a mere formality,
>   She likes a piquant jest.

She knows a thing
  or two or more,
You needn't say it
  twice,
Perhaps you've met
  that sort before—
She's naughty, but
  but she's nice!

" 'Her feelings are
  devotional
Toward Turkish
  cigarettes,
Impulsive and emo-
  tional,
She   loves   and
  smokes and bets,

She's played most every sort of game
    She doesn't take advice,
And people say — but just the same,
    She's naughty, but she's nice!

‘ “There isn’t much satiety
    When you’re around with her,   ‘
She’s brimming with variety,
    She’s different as it were;
And here’s to her, the patron saint
    Of cigarettes and dice,
She’s not demure nor shy nor quaint,
    She’s naughty — but she’s nice.’ ”

The Oracle looked at the row of “butts” on the ash
tray before him, sighed dubiously, then turned to the En-
gineer,—

‘ “A cigarette is the perfect type of a perfect pleasure,
it is exquisite and it leaves you unsatisfied,’ lend me the
materials, will you, McPherson? ”

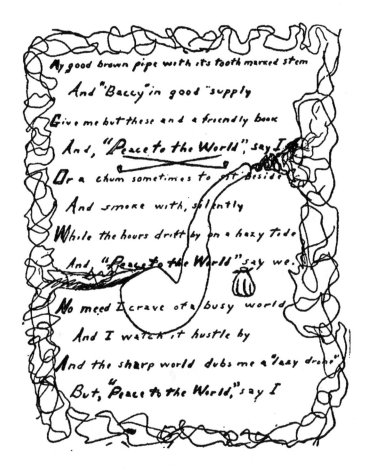

My good brown pipe with its tooth marked stem

And "Baccy" in good "supply

Give me but these and a friendly book

And, "Peace to the World", say I

Or a chum sometimes to sit beside

And smoke with, silently

While the hours drift by on a hazy tide

And, "Peace to the World" say we.

No need I crave of a busy world

And I watch it hustle by

And the sharp world dubs me a "lazy drone"

But, "Peace to the World," say I

MY OLD COB PIPE

You may talk about your cigarettes and fifty cent cigars,
Your water pipes and briars, and your meerchaums and the
     rest,
With your extra blend tobacco and your silver mounted
     jars,
But just and old-time corn cob pipe is what I love the best,
With some double charged tobacco that is strong and old
     and ripe,
And I'll get a whiff of heaven from my old cob pipe.

When the winter winds are shrieking and the snow drift
     blocks the door,
I take my old companion, and we settle by the fire,
And I tell my pipe my troubles, till they trouble me no
     more,
For he speaks a silent language and his sayings never tire,
He's a comforter and helper of a rare and valued type,
And the world has seemed the sweeter for my old cob pipe.

Oh he loves the books I care for, and I sometimes think
    he knows
How my Kipling stirs the spirit, how my Dobson warms
    the heart,
And the faithful spark within him like a distant camp fire
    glows,
When the masters swinging rhythm sings of field and town
    and mart.
Yes my pipe and I are comrades of a most congenial stripe
So I love and loaf and labor with my old cob pipe.

But most and best I love him when amidst his smoke I see
The vision of the maiden who is soon to be my wife,
Yet a little pang of sadness even then comes over me
Despite the gladsome promise of a happiness for life
And furtively from off my cheek a trickling tear I wipe,
For I've promised her to quit you now — my old cob pipe.

THE ORACLE ON MOODS

The room was in the usual smoke-house condition, with incense ascending from a collection of Durham-fed or Arcadia-filled pipes, from "home and tailor-made cigarettes," and from one lone cigar which pertained to the plutocrat of the crowd.

The Oracle surveyed the gang with satisfaction,

"Rather an intelligent audience I have tonight," he beamed, "not quite worthy to hear my utterances, of course, but fairly appreciative and not entirely obtuse; I am well pleased.

"My mood is most pleasurable tonight anyhow, and I am easily pleased, my gregarious instincts are dominant and it does me good to look upon the faces of both friend and foe, they all look good to me,— chuck the pained expression, well I ken that I have no foes in this bunch, you're all tolerant comrades whom I love much,— and this general feeling of good will which permeates me is mostly the result of my Lady Nicotine's gracious mood. She has today blessed my lot with flawless smokes; my pipes have been sweet and mellow, burning evenly with a gentle warmth and giving forth smoke which savors of the

sunny south whence the tobacco has come.   My cigar-
ettes have almost rolled themselves, not a paper has broken,
not a whiff but has been goodly.   The two cigars which
generous friends have this day given me were fat and
richly satisfying, and during all the hours no match has
failed in its incendiary duty.   I have been gorgeously happy
and without care.

"Such moods come but seldom, the gods dare not
make them more frequent lest many such plenteous hours
change us all to indolent though contented dawdlers.
Therefore the dieties usually incite her Nicotinian Lady-
ship to practice many an irritating caprice; our pipes grow
rank and our cigarettes part and disintegrate and no kind
friends come nigh with portly cigars.

"Sometimes these whims affect us not at all, or slightly,
and we dream our dreams or chat in utter obliviousness to
the guttering of ill-tempered pipes or the crumbling of
recalcitrant 'nails.'

"But oftenest these little rifts turn our souls bitter (I
know that figure is mixed), and amid the sour profanity
of our grouch the Lady Nicotine can soothe us not at all.

"Tonight, as I said before, *my* mood is as social as my
discourse is wandering, and the Lady has seen fit to make
the day tobaccistically perfect.   Tomorrow my mood may
be merely ruminant, in which case I shall wish only to be

alone with my visions, my reveries, my pipe and my to-
bacco jar, if one can be alone with such a plenitude of
companionship; and a day or two hence the mood may
again shift to the gregarious or at least the ' spoonarious,'
when I shall yearn to lounge at Her feet before the fire
and with no one to dispute or share my comfort, gaze up
at Her through the thin wreathes from my pipe.

" These are the smoker's moods, at any rate these are
mine, and though in my devious discursiveness tonight my
words seem without purpose, order or coherence; seem as
casual as the curls of smoke about our heads, nathless I
have spoken Truth, and if it be formless I care no jot,
since my day has been and is one of lazy content and idle
self-satisfaction.

" Now my dictums are done and we will close the day
with song.

    Smoke up! and care not for the past, it days are dead
        and done,
    Smoke up! nor heed the present for its skein is nearly
        spun.
    Smoke up! nor fear the future, for little gain is there —
    Smoke up! with good tobacco for it smothers all our
        care.''